The Heritage Foundation
LEADERSHIP FOR AMERICA

Changing America's Course

What's at stake in 2012

Washington's many pressures make it difficult for lawmakers to keep their focus. Thus, after electing them, it is essential that Americans hold lawmakers accountable. The Mandate for Leadership series provides an overview of the ideals that undergird sound policy on key issues and the main policy objectives that flow from them. It is a powerful tool to help responsible lawmakers turn principle into policy and a checklist for citizens to make sure that they do. *Changing America's Course* is the first product in Heritage's 2012 Mandate for Leadership series.

Changing America's Course

What's at stake in 2012

Foreword:
Ed Feulner, *President*

Executive Editor:
Matthew Spalding, *Vice President, American Studies and Director,*
B. Kenneth Simon Center for Principles and Politics

Contributors:
Saving the American Dream—Stuart Butler, *Distinguished Fellow and Director,*
Center for Policy Innovation; Alison Fraser, *Director, Thomas A. Roe Institute for*
Economic Policy Studies

Providing for the Common Defense—Kim Holmes, *Vice President, Foreign and*
Defense Policy Studies and Director, The Kathryn and Shelby Cullom Davis Institute
for International Studies; James Carafano, *Deputy Director, The Kathryn and Shelby*
Cullom Davis Institute for International Studies and Director, Douglas and Sarah
Allison Center for Foreign Policy Studies

Restoring Constitutional Government—Edwin Meese III, *Ronald Reagan*
Distinguished Fellow in Public Policy and Chairman of the Center for Legal & Judicial
Studies; Robert Alt, *Director, Rule of Law Programs and Senior Legal Fellow*

Table of Contents

Foreword

AMERICA TODAY FACES THREE OVER-arching challenges, each of which transcends the partisan divide and any one of which could cause grievous harm to our beloved country.

An entitlements challenge threatens economic prosperity for all, a defense challenge threatens our national security, and a constitutional challenge threatens the very meaning of this self-governing democracy. Faced with these looming problems, it is all too easy to lose hope and resign ourselves to a future of decline and mediocrity.

Americans have faced—and surmounted—similar challenges in the past, from the American Revolution to the Civil War, from World War II to the worldwide threat of Soviet communism. In each case, great leaders emerged and rallied the American people, and freedom emerged triumphant. Just as *Mandate for Leadership* played a significant role in launching the Reagan Revolution and so reviving the American spirit, so we hope that *Changing America's Course*, by pointing the way to a brighter future of opportunity and independence, will convince political leaders and concerned citizens alike that while our problems are quite serious if left unattended, they are by no means insurmountable once confronted by the indomitable character and unbounded strength of the American people.

— Ed Feulner, *President*

America's Choice

WE HAVE COME TO A TIME OF DECISION.

For far too long, the federal government has been on a binge of spending, taxing, and borrowing. It is bloated and vastly overextended, and its unsustainable promises now feed escalating debts that will cripple our economy, undermine our prosperity, and lead to fiscal insolvency.

At the same time, our political leaders defer our nation's security in a hostile and unstable world, neglecting their obligation to provide for the common defense and protect America's independence.

More than ever, the federal government operates far beyond its means and outside of its proper constitutional bounds, seemingly oblivious of its core functions. Endless rules and regulations touch every aspect of our daily life.

The United States is on the verge of becoming a country in decline—economically stagnant and debt-bound, heavily regulated and bureaucratic, unsure of its purpose and unconcerned about its freedom.

Are we at the end of the great American experiment in self-government?

This fate does not have to be our future. We can get spending under control, balance the budget, and shrink our debt—without raising taxes. We can assure

America's security, uphold the rule of law, and advance the cause of liberty in the world. We can reduce the size and scope of government and unleash the engines of economic productivity and the institutions of cultural renewal.

All of this is possible—but only if we take decisive action to fundamentally change our country's course and set America once again on the principled path of liberty, opportunity, and constitutional self-government.

An Exceptional Nation

Throughout history, as in many other parts of the world today, political rule was the privilege of the strongest or the most powerful. Property was the possession of kings, barons, and lords. Because wealth remained fixed in the hands of a very few, there was widespread poverty. Each was born to his or her destiny, and almost all were subject to someone else.

America is different. This nation is uniquely dedicated to the universal principles of human liberty: that all are fundamentally equal and equally endowed with unalienable rights to life, liberty, and the pursuit of happiness. Our government exists to secure these God-given rights, deriving its just powers from the consent of the governed. Our Constitution limits the power of government under the rule of law, creating a vigorous framework for expanding economic opportunity, protecting national independence, and securing liberty and justice for all.

These principles still define America as a nation and as a people. They explain why Americans look fondly to their nation's origins and remain fiercely patriotic, vigilantly assert their political rights and fulfill their civic responsibilities, constantly strive to live up to America's highest purposes and remain convinced of the special meaning of their country and its role in the world. It is why friends of freedom the world over look to the United States as an ally against tyrants and a powerful beacon for all of those who strive for liberty.

The American Dream

What matters in America is not where you come from but where you are going. That's because America's exceptional principles of liberty give rise to another characteristic unique to this country. We call it the American Dream.

That Americans are fundamentally equal and self-governing citizens, and that the United States government is limited to certain core functions, means that we have the liberty and opportunity to live our lives, control our fate, and pursue our happiness.

This nation is uniquely dedicated to the universal principles of human liberty: that all are fundamentally equal and equally endowed with unalienable rights to life, liberty, and the pursuit of happiness.

In the hands of the American people, the principles proclaimed in the Declaration of Independence and promulgated in the United States Constitution have created a nation unlike any other in history. Its economy produces almost a quarter of the world's wealth, and its military forces remain the most powerful on the globe. The institutions of civil society—family, church, school, and private associations—thrive in America, forming an independent people that are among the most hard-working, church-going, generous, and forward-looking in the world.

The principle that each has a right to the rewards of his own labor—the promise that you can keep what you earn and that what you save and acquire is your property—forms a dynamic society in which every member can work hard, pursue opportunity, and advance in life based on individual talent and ability. In America, earned success corresponds to merit and industriousness rather than to aristocratic privilege and inheritance.

The monumental achievement of this great country is that it makes comfort and general affluence, safety and security, self-government and the blessings of liberty—all traditionally the province of the privileged class—available to the whole of society. It is the potent combination of political liberty under the rule of law, the endless creativity of the marketplace, and the enduring moral character of the American people that assures opportunity for all and fuels the unlimited promises of America.

A Failed Social Experiment

About a hundred years ago, there arose a different dream: that a better society could be engineered by government.

Early progressive reformers were convinced that the American Founders were wrong about man and the necessity of limited government. Instead, they believed that government could reshape society and rid it of the diversities and inequalities that had been unleashed by individual liberty, the flourishing of free enterprise, and the resulting growth of commerce and business. A more activist government, built on evolving rights and a "living" Constitution, would redistribute wealth and level out differences in society through taxation, regulation, and social-welfare programs, all centrally administered by the federal government.

While the new construct was designed during the Progressive Era, it began to take its current form under the New Deal. In order to "assure us equality in the pursuit of happiness," Franklin D. Roosevelt proposed a Second Bill of Rights, guaranteeing to all Americans a useful job, a living wage, adequate health care, a good education, decent housing, and retirement security. Lyndon Johnson's Great Society radicalized the argument by asserting that the purpose of government is the assurance of equal outcomes—"not just equality as a *right* and a *theory*," as Johnson once put it, "but equality as a *fact* and equality as a *result*." By creating a truly national bureaucracy of open-ended programs in housing, education, the environment, urban renewal, and even the arts and humanities—not to mention its "War on Poverty"—the Great Society and its progeny in both political parties effected the greatest expansion and centralization of government in American history.

And so was born the modern, ever-growing welfare state.

The current Administration under President Barack Obama has launched a new era of liberal reform and revived the old statist model: the transformation of a Troubled Asset Relief Program into a government slush fund to bail out banks and car companies, a massive "stimulus" bill based on the discredited theory that government spending rather than private markets creates economic growth, the most significant expansion of financial regulations since the New Deal, and the creation of an extensive new entitlement program that regulates the entire health care sector. All is to be solved by government through more government.

The Patient Protection and Affordable Care Act—better known as Obamacare—is the centerpiece of this agenda. Massive regulatory authority over one-sixth of the American economy will be transferred to a collection of over 150 federal agencies, bureaus, and commissions along with an unprecedented delegation of power to the Secretary of Health and Human Services. Nothing will be allowed outside of the new regulatory framework—no independent state programs, no individuals or businesses permitted not to participate, no true private market alternatives. The requirement for individuals to buy insurance is both unprecedented and unconstitutional: If government can regulate inactivity, it can do anything.

In this world, a new governing class of experts and political elites insists on enforcing their views of political and economic "fairness" rather than letting us govern ourselves under the rule of law, seizing the opportunities of free enterprise and shaped by a flourishing civil society. Such limitless authority leads inevitably to bureaucratic favoritism, inequalities based on special interests and undue political influence, and the crony corruption of picking winners and losers.

Shattered Dreams, Broken Promises
Despite its good intentions, liberalism's grand experiment threatens to turn America into a very different country, more like the failing states of old Europe. The costs and burdens of our current trajectory are staggering:

- **Government spending is out of control.** Annual federal spending has increased by 289 percent since 1970 (after adjusting for inflation), nearly 12 times faster than median household income. Total annual federal spending did not reach $1 trillion until 1973 but exceeded $2 trillion less than 20 years later and first topped $3 trillion in 2008. Total federal spending in the United States now exceeds 24 percent of the economy.

- **Dependence on government is growing rapidly.** More than 70 percent of federal spending goes to dependence programs. More

CHART 1

The Current and Future Crisis: Runaway Federal Spending Will Result in Huge Budget Deficits

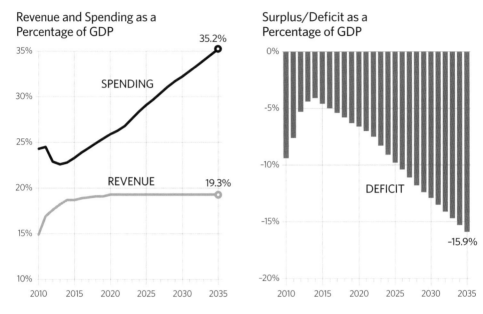

Revenue and Spending as a Percentage of GDP

SPENDING — 35.2%

REVENUE — 19.3%

Surplus/Deficit as a Percentage of GDP

DEFICIT — -15.9%

Source: Heritage Foundation calculations based on data from Congressional Budget Office, Alternative Fiscal Scenario.

than 67.3 million Americans—*approaching a quarter of our fellow citizens*—now rely on assistance from the federal government for housing, food, income, health and retirement support, or other assistance once considered to be the responsibility of individuals, families, neighborhoods, churches, and other civil society institutions. Dependence on government has increased 23 percent since 2008.

- **Liberalism's promises are unsustainable.** Over the next 25 years, more than 77 million baby boomers—the largest generational retirement in world history—will begin collecting Social Security checks, drawing Medicare benefits, and relying on long-term care under Medicaid. Now more than half of all federal program spending, the cost of guaranteed entitlements is expected to nearly double over the next decade. Without major reforms, entitlement spending will consume all federal tax revenues by 2045.

- **America faces a debt crisis.** Publicly held debt now tops $11 trillion—about $36,000 for every American. This is nearly three-fourths the size of the entire American economy. Over the next 10 years, it will exceed the size of our economy, and by 2036, it will be nearly twice the size of our economy. This is before the long-term costs of entitlements (like Medicare, Medicaid, or Social Security) are added to the ledger.

- **Future generations will be shackled with massive and unbearable social burdens.** Americans face $45.9 trillion in unfunded obligations (what we have promised to pay) for Social Security and Medicare alone over the next 75 years. That is more than $200,000 for every American of working age or younger—a massive level of debt that is sure to slow the economy and could force even higher rates of taxation in the future.

The massive expansion of the regulatory side of the modern state—over 3,500 new regulations just last year—makes this all the worse. In its first three years, the Obama Administration imposed 106 major new rules, each increasing regulatory burdens by $100 million or more, 28 in the past year. These new rules impose over $46 billion in new costs on Americans annually, plus another $11 billion in one-time implementation costs. Estimated to cost over $1.75 trillion a year, the overall regulatory burden weakens the American economy, impedes job creation, and undermines America's competitive position in the world.

We need a fundamental correction of our nation's potentially fatal path.

We can see the effect of all this in the status of our economic freedom relative to that of other countries. Recent government interventions have eroded limits on government. Public spending by all levels of government now exceeds 40 percent of total domestic output. The regulatory burden on business continues to increase rapidly, and heightened uncertainty further increases regulations' negative impact. As a result, according to the *Index of Economic Freedom* compiled by The Heritage Foundation and *The Wall Street Journal*,

America has declined among nations from fourth place in 2007 to sixth place in 2009 to 10th place in 2012. Today, the United States is only "mostly free" when it comes to economic freedom.

The result is that a limited government designed to secure our right to the pursuit of happiness and to break down unjust barriers to opportunity now subsidizes mediocrity, penalizes success, and has become the chief barrier to achieving individual opportunity and national prosperity.

Obama's dream has become America's nightmare of broken promises, endless debts, and lost hopes.

Changing America's Course

Many have long maintained that the modern state is inevitable, permanent, and ever-expanding. Stewardship of big government and incremental reforms around its edges are seen as the only practical options. Our governing elites try to make government more efficient, more frugal, and more compassionate, but they never question its overall direction. Today, however, it is precisely the direction in which we are headed that must be forthrightly challenged.

There is widespread recognition of the overwhelming problems we face, and there is a mounting realization of the only way out: *America must decisively change course, and it must do so now.*

This is not the time for tinkering or for timidity. We must not be distracted by the political skirmishes of the moment. We need a fundamental correction of our nation's potentially fatal path.

America urgently needs clear ideas, honest answers, and bold reforms that meet the demands of the moment and address the magnitude of the challenges before us. Such actions—and only such actions—will bring the new era of prosperity, security, and self-government that is required to save our country.

— Matthew Spalding, *Executive Editor*

Saving the American Dream

THE IMMEDIATE AND LIFE-THREATENING challenge is to get our fiscal house in order. We face a staggering fiscal problem that threatens the very future of our nation. At the same time, we must also keep our core obligations and commitments to the American people and restore opportunity and prosperity for all.

According to the Declaration of Independence, all are endowed with unalienable rights to life, liberty, and the pursuit of happiness. Just as the pursuit of happiness is the purpose of liberty, the opportunity to earn and attain the material goods that contribute to that happiness is the practical expression of that pursuit.

When it comes to the economy, the primary obligation of the federal government is to secure equally the rights of all, destroy barriers to opportunity, and uphold the rule of law. As a result of economic reward being available to all, there is an incentive to earn more, save more, and invest in more opportunities for the future—which encourages enterprise and economic activity. For those who cannot care for themselves, there is a basic safety net formed by the active involvement of civil society and public assistance at the appropriate level of government.

But most important, the ladder of opportunity is available for *everyone* to work, prosper, and make a better life. Vastly diminished, poverty is no longer a permanent condition from which there is no hope of escape.

Rather than the guarantor of economic outcomes, government should be the sturdy framework for opportunity, economic growth, and human flourishing. It should remove unfair obstacles to economic markets, break down artificial structures that prevent competition, and otherwise keep tax rates low, reduce government spending, and prevent the overregulation of private enterprise. Such an economic program would bring better options, greater opportunity, and higher rewards to those who work and create wealth, thereby stimulating the overall economy and providing more jobs and greater prosperity for everyone.

How to Save the American Dream

The underlying problem today is that for too long, the federal government has been living beyond the means of the American people. Congress after Congress has made unwise and unaffordable promises. Massive government spending and surging debt threaten to destroy the foundations of our economy and steal the American Dream from our children and grandchildren. Not only will we continue to struggle with huge federal deficits in the near term, but the problem will become ever larger and more suffocating in the decades to come. If entitlements are not reformed, the next generation and future ones will have to pay punitive tax rates and sustain debt burdens that will significantly restrain their liberty.

We must tackle the root of the spending problem by renegotiating the unsustainable entitlement promises that are overwhelming us. If we act soon rather than waiting until the problem is too urgent and too big to fix prudently, we can address the problems in ways that actually strengthen economic security.

Reforming entitlement programs is only half of the economic security equation. The other half is to allow the American spirit of self-reliance to flourish and to cast off the growing and dispiriting dependence on government that has characterized recent decades. Faster growth through greater economic freedom will enable more and more Americans to build both a solid and secure life and retirement for themselves and the means, as a community, to help those who worked hard but do not have the means to support themselves in retirement.

To ensure prosperity and growth for ourselves and our children, we must reduce the federal government so that it is closer to its proper size and focus it on performing its core constitutional functions. This will mean deep and sustained reductions in federal spending and a refocusing of that spending. We must also hold down taxes while reforming our needlessly complex, burdensome, and highly unfair tax system to sharpen incentives and reward saving. We must re-energize entrepreneurs and workers to restore America's prosperity powerhouse. In the end, we can best solve our spending and debt problem through the growth, opportunity, and prosperity that come with low tax rates and limited government.

Saving the American Dream is The Heritage Foundation's plan to fix the debt, cut spending, and restore prosperity. Under the plan, we would achieve balance in the federal budget within 10 years and do so at a maximum level of taxes and spending that Americans have indicated they are prepared to accept if the economy is strong (about 18.5 percent of GDP). Not only that, but the plan maintains balance at that level permanently, together with a large tax cut when compared with current tax projections.

We can achieve this result because the plan maintains three strategies in parallel. One is to reform the tax system to spur solid economic growth and build up household savings for future needs, including retirement. Another is to cut regular spending quickly and deeply while selling off government assets that should be in private hands, such as surplus buildings and land. And third, at the same time these shorter-term cuts are happening, the plan begins important structural reforms in the major entitlement programs like Social Security and Medicare. These changes yield small savings initially, but over time, as the reforms gradually take effect, they produce the large future savings needed to maintain permanent balance at a reasonable level of total federal spending.

Here are the core elements of the *Saving the American Dream* plan.

Health Care for Families

Health care costs are rising at an alarming rate, while individuals and families have less control over their health care dollars or decisions. Worse still, the recently enacted Patient Protection and Affordable Care Act (Obamacare) is accelerating these problems. In sharp contrast to the centralized government approach of the Obama legislation, what America needs is a consumer-centered, market-based approach to reduce health care costs and give patients and their families a greater say in health care spending and decisions that affect their lives.

For numerous reasons—its massive costs, regulatory overreach, and constitutional deformity for starters—the first thing to do is repeal Obamacare, removing an immense burden on the American economy before it does any more damage. Only then can we pursue real, market-based health care reform in the United States.

America needs a consumer-centered, market-based approach to reduce health care costs and give patients and their families a greater say in health care spending and decisions that affect their lives.

The Heritage Foundation has long recommended major health care reform to create a health care system that assures Americans' access to affordable health care services. This system is based on consumer choice and personal ownership of coverage, together with a competitive infrastructure led by state-based market reforms and innovation.

Saving the American Dream includes overall key budget and tax components of the Heritage health care reform, including reform of the tax treatment of health insurance and assistance for lower-income families:

- It provides a health insurance tax credit of $2,000 for individuals and $3,500 for families—far more help than under current law. Americans can use this credit to help pay for an insurance plan that their employer offers, or they can use it to buy insurance outside the workplace.

- Low-income Americans will receive federal assistance that mirrors the tax credit to buy the same health insurance as those with middle and higher incomes—allowing Medicaid recipients a better quality option. Very low-income families with children receive additional assistance for health care coverage, worth as much as $9,000 per year.

- By 2014, the Heritage plan puts Medicaid on a fiscally sustainable path while giving states greater latitude to develop innovative ways to reduce costs and improve health care for the poor elderly and disabled.

These and other health insurance reforms will promote competition, drive down costs, and give Americans the finest health care system in the world without bankrupting America.

Today, Social Security and Medicare provide heavily subsidized benefits to everyone, regardless of their need. This has become utterly unaffordable.

Reforming America's Retirement Programs

In addition to the Medicaid entitlement, the major entitlement programs for retirees—Social Security and Medicare—must also be reformed. Decades ago, politicians from both parties promised baby boomers health and retirement benefits but provided no way to pay for them. Now we are faced with the consequences of their neglect—a staggering fiscal problem that threatens the very future of our nation. Medicare and Social Security face nearly $40 trillion in long-term unfunded obligations—over $200,000 for every non-elderly American.

Reforming America's entitlement programs for seniors means redesigning them to refocus them on achieving their proper goal of providing real economic security without passing a crushing financial burden on to younger generations. Today, Social Security and Medicare provide heavily subsidized benefits to everyone, regardless of their need. This has become utterly unaffordable.

We need to transform these programs into real insurance. That means the government would provide much better protection for everyone against the potential of severe medical and financial problems during retirement but would not provide generous benefits to those who do not need them. Meanwhile, other reforms would encourage working Americans to build a retirement nest egg and obtain insurance for retirement so that they reduce their dependence on government during their senior years.

Here is how *Saving the American Dream* proposes to reform Social Security:

- In keeping with the approach of real insurance, Social Security will gradually be transformed from an "income replacement" system back to its original purpose of guaranteeing seniors freedom from fear of poverty and assuring a decent retirement income. This means that basic Social Security benefits will evolve over time into a flat payment that is sufficient to keep them out of poverty throughout their retirement rather than a payment based on lifetime earnings.

- Because the new Social Security is more like a real insurance system, designed to protect seniors from poverty, retirees with high incomes from sources other than Social Security will receive a smaller check, and very affluent seniors will receive no check.

- Americans live much longer than they used to, and the cost of many years of benefits plays a major role in Social Security's financial problems. For this reason, the Social Security (and Medicare) retirement ages will be raised gradually and then indexed to life expectancy. This will create a more reasonable balance between the number of years a person works and the number of years one receives Social Security benefits.

- At the same time the retirement programs are scaled back and focused, the plan uses tax policy and other steps to boost savings and so create a more solid foundation of financial security and reduce dependence on the federal government.

This new Social Security system is reasonable, predictable, and affordable. It focuses resources on those who need the most help while providing complete protection against poverty for all seniors who qualify for full benefits.

Saving the American Dream encourages far greater economic growth by lowering rates and removing multiple layers of taxation on the same income.

Here is how *Saving the American Dream* proposes to reform Medicare:

- Under the plan, Medicare also becomes more like real insurance, including true protection against bankruptcy from medical bills— a protection that Medicare does not include today.

- Medicare will be required to operate within a true long-term budget. Today, it is an open-ended entitlement with no real budget, which is why Medicare currently is projected to impose almost $37 trillion in unfunded obligations onto our children and grandchildren.

- To make this program affordable, each retiree will be given control of his or her share of the true budget, using it to pick the coverage that's right for the retiree, not coverage that is designed by a bureaucrat.

- In order to reach a balanced budget without tax increases, very high-income seniors will receive a smaller amount of budget money to pay for their coverage. The most affluent of all will continue to have the insurance protection of Medicare but will pay the full cost themselves.

CHART 2

The Heritage Plan Would Rein in Mandatory Entitlement Spending

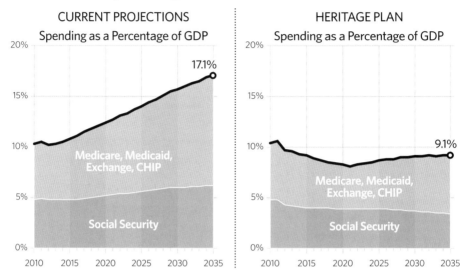

CURRENT PROJECTIONS
Spending as a Percentage of GDP

17.1%

Medicare, Medicaid, Exchange, CHIP

Social Security

HERITAGE PLAN
Spending as a Percentage of GDP

9.1%

Medicare, Medicaid, Exchange, CHIP

Social Security

Sources: Current projections: Heritage Foundation calculations based on data from Congressional Budget Office, Alternative Fiscal Scenario. Heritage Plan: Calculations by the Center for Data Analysis, The Heritage Foundation, based on baseline data in the current projections, data provided by the Peter G. Peterson Foundation, and CDA policy models.

- The plan abolishes government restrictions on the ability of doctors and their patients who are on Medicare to agree to services and payments that are different from those prescribed under Medicare. So *Saving the American Dream* restores the freedom of contract for doctors and their patients.

Stopping Uncontrolled Government Spending

It is also vital that we rein in government's uncontrolled spending. Although the major entitlement programs are the primary driver of long-term spending and debt, Congress must take tough action on discretionary programs and smaller entitlement programs to reach a balanced budget and ensure that federal spending is smaller, more effective, and more efficient. Rather than across-the-board spending reductions, which would not set true priorities for government, *Saving the American Dream* proposes six guidelines for reform:

- The federal government should focus on performing a limited number of appropriate governmental duties well while empowering state and local governments, which are closer to the people, to address local needs creatively.

- Functions that the private sector can perform more efficiently should be transferred to the private sector.

- Duplicative programs should be consolidated both to save money and to improve government assistance.

- Federal programs should more precisely target those who are actually in need, which means reducing aid to large businesses and upper-income individuals who do not need taxpayer assistance and enforcing program eligibility rules better.

- Outdated and ineffective programs should be eliminated.

- Waste, fraud, and abuse should be cleaned up wherever found.

Reforms that follow these guidelines will produce a more effective and efficient government and promote stronger economic growth. Reducing the size and scope of the federal government would increase the role of the states and the marketplace in choosing their own practices, bringing decision-making closer to the people and away from unelected government administrators.

Tax Reform for Economic Growth

Finally, to expand jobs and opportunity, the American tax system needs fundamental reform as well. *Saving the American Dream* proposes transforming the current tax system into a modern flat tax that taxes individual income only once and replaces all federal income taxes, all payroll taxes, the death tax, and virtually all excise taxes.

For individuals, the current system should be replaced with a new flat-rate tax applied to income after deducting all savings and investment. Taxable income should be reduced by the net amount contributed to savings and investment,

CHART 3

The Heritage Plan Simplifies the Tax System and Lowers Taxes

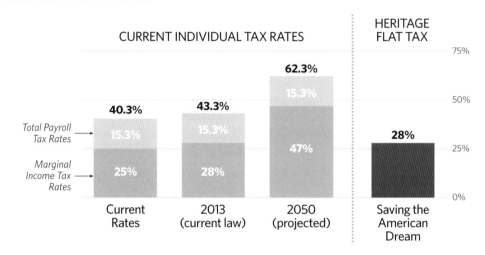

CURRENT INDIVIDUAL TAX RATES			HERITAGE FLAT TAX

Total Payroll Tax Rates →

Marginal Income Tax Rates →

	Current Rates	2013 (current law)	2050 (projected)	Saving the American Dream
Total	40.3%	43.3%	62.3%	28%
Payroll	15.3%	15.3%	15.3%	
Income	25%	28%	47%	

Sources: Congressional Budget Office, Tax Foundation. Heritage Plan: Calculations by the Center for Data Analysis.

---

which should be taxable only when spent. This eliminates double taxation of savings and ensures that individuals pay taxes only on what they withdraw from the economy and not on savings that they make available for investment in the economy by others.

Today's business tax code should be replaced by a flat business tax on income from domestic sales of goods and services with deductions for labor costs and purchases from other businesses, including expensing of capital purchases. All business activity, including corporate, should be taxed under the new flat business tax.

We must fix the labyrinth of complexities and inequities that taxpayers must endure in today's system by replacing it with a new system that is flat, simple, and transparent. *Saving the American Dream* encourages far greater economic growth by lowering rates and removing multiple layers of taxation on the same income. One low rate replacing today's array of income and payroll tax rates would treat all businesses the same and allow them to compete better globally. We should end today's disincentives to build savings—whether for retirement or for buying a house—by taxing only income that is spent on consumption so that Americans can build better economic security for themselves and their families. And we can do all this without raising taxes by injecting every dollar saved back into the economy through lower rates, not so-called deficit reduction.

Overall, *Saving the American Dream* gets us back to the level of taxes Americans historically have been willing to pay during a strong economy—18.5 percent of the economy—and caps taxes at that level. More important, under such a plan, working Americans will have far greater economic freedom, more opportunities, more jobs, and higher incomes.

The Imperative of Reform

Fundamental budget, fiscal, and regulatory reform is imperative to prevent national bankruptcy and permanent economic stagnation. *Saving the American Dream* balances the budget within 10 years and keeps it balanced thereafter while providing greater protection for poor and senior Americans. By reducing government benefits to the wealthiest Americans while not increasing taxes, these reforms immediately begin reducing deficits that threaten the economy. They reduce the federal government to its core functions and responsibilities. And they responsibly address ruinous public debt that will otherwise overwhelm not only ourselves, but also our children and grandchildren. In doing these things, we can save the American Dream for future generations.

Providing for the Common Defense

DESPITE THE GRAVE FISCAL CHALLENGE WE face, we must remain ever vigilant in an increasingly dangerous world, defending ourselves, securing our independence, and strengthening the cause of liberty.

In the Declaration of Independence, the right of the people to institute government means "laying its foundations on such principles and organizing its powers in such form, as to them shall seem most likely to effect their *safety* and *happiness*." Happiness is the objective, but safety is the initial requirement of its pursuit. Collective defense against external threats is the primary reason why the American colonies banded together in the first place. A chief purpose of the Constitution—and the particular obligation of the federal government—is to provide for the common defense.

It is the constitutional duty of the federal government to secure the country's international borders and preserve and protect its territorial integrity, to strengthen and preserve its constitutional government, and to promote the long-term prosperity and well-being of its people. This means that the United States must be able, willing, and prepared at all times to defend itself, its people, and its institutions from conventional and unconventional threats to its vital interests, both at home and abroad.

At the same time, by the very nature of the principles upon which it is established, the United States, more than any other nation in history, has an obligation to uphold and advance liberty. A profound commitment to the concept of sovereignty must be at the center of our nation's policies. But liberty does not belong only to this country. The United States must continue to recognize its special responsibility to defend the cause of liberty in the world.

Managed Decline?

In recent years, despite unmatched rates of spending and government activity, the federal government has been doing less and less to fulfill its core responsibility of national defense.

Defense spending is near historical lows. Whether considered as a percentage of our economy or of the federal budget, the share that is spent by the Department of Defense is declining. From a high of 36.3 percent of GDP during World War II, 11.7 percent during the Korean War, and 8.9 percent during the Vietnam War, general defense spending has fallen from 6 percent during the Reagan Administration and 4.6 percent during the first Bush Administration. The budget for all defense spending in fiscal year (FY) 2011 was 4.7 percent. If the Administration's current plans to cut defense succeed, that percentage will drop to 3 percent or lower.

The root of the problem lies in decisions made in the 1990s. After the fall of the Berlin Wall, Presidents George H. W. Bush and Bill Clinton cut defense spending dramatically. During the Cold War, U.S. military strategy called for the ability to fight and win two major wars and one "brushfire" conflict simultaneously. With the collapse of the Soviet Union, that capability was sharply reduced in order to give the American people a "peace dividend." The Clinton Administration reduced the entire military—its forces and equipment—by fully one-third under the utopian assumption that the end of the Cold War would lead to a "lasting peace."

President Ronald Reagan's military buildup in the 1980s, coupled with his successful diplomacy, created a cushion that largely allowed defense investments to be deferred in the 1990s even as military operations increased.

Temporary defense budget increases in the aftermath of the terrorist attacks of 9/11 have been mostly consumed by an increased pace of military activities worldwide. The ongoing need to invest in and modernize the force—new planes, ships, weapon systems, and equipment—remains and is growing more urgent.

On average, major U.S. military platforms are now more than 25 years old and are wearing out much more quickly than planned. The combat vehicle fleet of Abrams tanks, for instance, is largely based on technology from the 1980s and earlier. The average age of the Air Force's inventory exceeds that of many of its pilots.

At the end of the Cold War, the Army was cut from 18 divisions to 10, and ever since then, it has operated short on basic equipment. Our soldiers have been stretched and strained by 10 years of combat in Iraq and Afghanistan. The Air Force is smaller than it has been since Pearl Harbor but is flying more missions than ever. Today's Navy is smaller than it has been since 1916, yet it is being tasked with more responsibilities than ever, such as securing vital sea-lanes of commerce.

The bipartisan Quadrennial Defense Review (QDR) Independent Panel concluded in 2010 that "the aging of the inventories and equipment used by the services, the decline in the size of the Navy, escalating personnel entitlements, overhead and procurement costs, and the growing stress on the force means that a train wreck is coming in the areas of personnel, acquisition, and force structure." This "train wreck" is here, and it threatens to undermine America's ability to defend itself and protect its vital national interests at a time when threats to its security are increasing.

And yet, consider the state of our nation's current defense budgeting:

- When calculating from his fiscal year 2013 budget request, President Obama is proposing to reduce total defense spending to $566.3 billion (in budget authority) in FY 2014. This compares to an actual defense spending figure in FY 2010 of $721.3 billion. Thus, he is proposing to bring the defense spending level down by $155 billion—over 21 percent—in just four years.

- This does not account for the effects of inflation. If inflation is factored in, the defense spending level reduction over the same period will be about 27 percent. In the fiscal years following 2014 out to 2022, President Obama proposes to keep total defense spending at the $566.3 billion level, as adjusted at a rate marginally higher than the rate of inflation. Even in current dollar terms, the total defense spending level in FY 2022 will be well below what it was in FY 2010.

- Further, President Obama's budget proposal ignores the requirement for "sequestration" of the defense budget under the Budget Control Act of 2011. Sequestration will shave an additional roughly $50 billion off the defense budget in FY 2014, thereby bringing the number down to about $516 billion. This will be a 28 percent reduction in current-dollar terms or a 33 percent reduction in inflation-adjusted dollars over the four-year period from FY 2010–FY 2014. Sequestration will impose the same roughly $50 billion reduction from the President's already reduced requested level in each of the fiscal years 2015 through 2021.

It is extremely unrealistic to think that the United States can cut defense spending levels by about one-third from the 2010 level and keep them at roughly this level in terms of inflation-adjusted dollars over the remainder of the 10-year period and still maintain its current, already diminished level of commitment to the nation's security and international obligations. To meet these cuts, at least one and possibly two Navy carrier strike groups will disappear. A large part of the U.S. missile defense program will have to be scaled back, exposing millions of Americans unnecessarily to nuclear attack. America's ability to maintain combat-ready, forward-deployed units around the world will be diminished. Overseas bases will have to be shut down, meaning that it will be far more expensive and take far longer to move U.S. forces where they need to be in the future—assuming they can even get there at all.

Historical experience and recent events suggest that the world is not about to become any less dangerous and unpredictable. Yet the current Administration lays out long-range cuts in programs that could take years or even decades to

CHART 4

National Defense Spending Would Plummet Under Obama's Budget

President Obama's "lean defense" strategy would create a hollow force and exacerbate today's readiness crisis. Decreases in funding for the core defense program mean losing capabilities that are crucial for the military to fulfill its constitutional duty to provide for the common defense.

Percentage of GDP

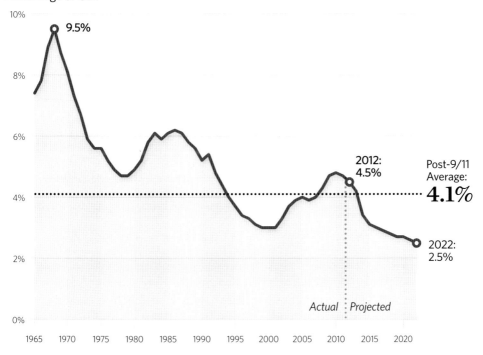

Source: Office of Management and Budget.

reverse. President Obama assures us that his defense budget will "maintain our military superiority with armed forces that are agile, flexible and ready for the full range of contingencies and threats." How so? Because the "tide of war" is allegedly receding for the United States and our military.

This is a recipe not for trimming waste but for significantly reducing our military's operational capacity. From a policy perspective, this is a strategy of managed decline.

The Common Defense

Some claim that excessive defense spending is responsible for our government's fiscal crisis. This is simply false. Today, we spend a total of about 5 percent of gross domestic product (GDP) on defense. By comparison, spending on Social Security, Medicare, and Medicaid has grown from 2.5 percent of GDP in 1965 to roughly 10 percent today—and these entitlements are projected to absorb all federal revenue by 2045. The President's defense budget, even when coupled with the automatic defense spending cuts required by the 2011 Budget Control Act, will *not* solve America's fiscal crisis. It will, however, drastically reduce America's ability to deter aggression around the world.

To protect and defend America's vital national interests, the U.S. military must have the tools it needs to deter attacks and enhance diplomatic efforts—and, when diplomacy and deterrence fail, to fight and win conflicts.

Government spending, massive bloat, and constitutional overreach must be on the chopping block. But the core and undisputed constitutional responsibility of the United States government to provide for the common defense—especially at a time when we should be seriously thinking about our strategy and vital interests in an increasingly dangerous world—must not be up for negotiation.

America's armed forces are the safeguard of our nation's liberties and an instrument of freedom and security, providing for the common defense of the United States by protecting the homeland and securing America's interests abroad. The vital national interests of the United States have remained remarkably consistent, especially since World War II: safeguarding our national security; preventing a major power threat to Europe, East Asia, or the Persian Gulf; maintaining access to foreign trade and the resources essential to national and economic security; and protecting Americans against threats to their lives and well-being.

CHART 5

Medicare and Other Entitlements Are Crowding Out Spending on Defense

Ever-increasing entitlement spending is putting pressure on key spending priorities, such as national defense, a core constitutional function of government. Defense spending has declined significantly over time, even when the wars in Iraq and Afghanistan are included, as spending on the three major entitlements—Social Security, Medicare, and Medicaid—has more than tripled.

Percentage of GDP

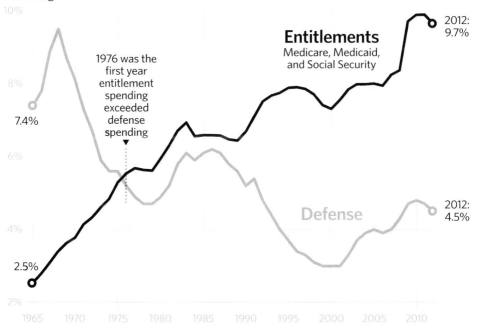

Note: 2012 figures estimated.

Source: Office of Management and Budget.

The mission of the United States military is determined by America's vital interests and an assessment of the threats to those interests. This drives force structure requirements: how many brigades, wings, carrier groups, and other military assets are needed, where they are deployed, and how they are used. Force requirements and capabilities in service to the military's overall strategic mission should determine the budget and spending needs for national defense.

What threats do we face? Both Iran and North Korea have active nuclear and ballistic missile programs and the ability to reach U.S. allies and forward-deployed troops with ballistic missiles. China is engaged in a non-transparent major military buildup with unclear intentions. A re-emergent Russia is vigorously modernizing its nuclear forces and seeks to intimidate its neighbors, Europe, and the NATO alliance. Terrorist threats to the U.S. and its European allies emanate from Southwest Asia, the Middle East, and various failed states. Cyber attacks threaten critical financial and communication networks in our economy and throughout society, as well as the national security assets that protect us.

Outsourcing American leadership will not solve our problems or meet the many challenges to liberty.

Declining defense investments that force America to the margins of military superiority—while countries like China and Russia invest heavily to modernize and expand their forces and rogue states like Iran and North Korea develop their nuclear weapons programs—are risky and dangerous. To protect and defend America's vital national interests, the U.S. military must have the tools it needs to deter attacks and enhance diplomatic efforts—and, when diplomacy and deterrence fail, to fight and win conflicts. Combat victory requires a force adequately equipped to defend the U.S. and its allies against strategic attacks, to prevail in traditional and asymmetrical warfare, to defeat terrorist organizations, and to respond to threats that emanate from failed states.

What steps must the United States take to provide for the common defense?

- **Pursue efficiency and eliminate wasteful spending.** Congress must pursue efficiency and reform efforts and work to eliminate waste in the defense budget. Roughly $100 billion in savings can be achieved in the near term by continuing select efficiency initiatives undertaken by former Secretary of Defense Robert Gates, implementing select reforms recommended by the National Commission on Fiscal Responsibility and Reform, expanding the use of public–private partnerships for performance-based logistics, modernizing base operations and the maintenance and supply systems, reducing wear and tear on military equipment, and increasing the use of multiyear contracts. These savings should be reinvested in defense modernization.

- **Modernize the force structure.** The U.S. needs a modernized force structure that matches both America's security commitments and the security threats that it faces. This will require a procurement spending level 1.5 times the current amount spent on research and development, focusing on key modernization programs like the F-35 Joint Strike Fighter and *Virginia*-class submarine as well as new long-range strike assets and next-generation attack helicopters. To address growing concerns in Asia, the U.S. must fund the modernization of its surface fleet.

- **Pursue missile defense.** The growing threat from long-range nuclear missiles endangers the lives of millions of Americans and upsets regional and global stability. America needs a comprehensive ballistic missile defense capability that employs a multilayered system of sea, ground, air, and space-based systems. To protect Americans effectively against rogue attacks in the near future, a rigorous program of testing, development, and deployment of missile defenses must be adequately funded.

- **Fund the core defense budget.** To ensure that the nation's military forces have what they need to do their task, the core defense budget should be funded by an average of $720 billion from FY 2012 to FY 2016 (in addition to funding our ongoing contingency operations). This level is not only reasonable; it is also affordable, amounting to around 4 percent of GDP—far less than the average of 7.5 percent spent on defense since World War II. This commitment would enable the U.S. to maintain stable troop levels in an all-volunteer force, provide sufficient readiness funds, and ensure adequate funding for research and development and procurement in order to modernize America's conventional and strategic forces.

The Doctrine of Doubt

Behind liberalism's blueprint for national decline is a deep sense of doubt about America and its purpose.

Does America's dedication to universal principles of liberty give it any special responsibilities in the world? In the debate over American exceptionalism, President Obama is dismissive: "I believe in American exceptionalism, just as I suspect that the Brits believe in British exceptionalism and the Greeks believe in Greek exceptionalism." Such doubt about America's purpose and liberty's obligations—whether by the progressive Left or the isolationist Right—undermines America's security and leadership in the world.

Without principled American leadership, the world will become a more dangerous place— for Americans and for freedom.

Throughout his tenure, President Obama has laid out in public statements the tenets of a doctrine that purports to remake America simply as one nation among many, approaching other nations with no singular claim either to responsibility or exceptionalism. This President believes that America should adopt a more modest attitude in state-to-state relations, play a more restrained role on the world stage, look more to international organizations, and place greater emphasis on diplomacy and "soft power."

The tenets of the Obama Doctrine will have both intended and unintended consequences: They make America less confident in itself by encouraging self-doubt, and they will make us less secure as other countries feel emboldened to threaten us and hold our policies in contempt. Outsourcing American leadership will not solve our problems or meet the many challenges to liberty.

American policy must not be driven either by the naïve notion that we can rid the world of tyranny and remake other nations in our image or by foolish claims that we can somehow withdraw from the world and isolate ourselves from threats to our sovereignty and independence. The better course—consistent with constitutional government, under which elected leaders have an obligation to act in the best interests of the people they represent and on whose behalf they exercise power—is to focus on America's vital national interests in light of its principles, maintaining the United States' freedom of action while prudently advancing liberty in the world.

A Renewed American Leadership

A strong and confident America should reassert American leadership in defense of U.S. vital national interests and liberty around the world by:

- **Maintaining the fight against terrorism.** The war on terrorism is not over. America must continue to adapt to ever-changing terrorist threats by preserving existing counterterrorism and intelligence tools (such as the PATRIOT Act), holding countries accountable for their support of terrorists, and addressing the threat posed by state-sponsored terrorism. The U.S. must win the war of ideas against Islamist extremist ideology both at home and abroad.

- **Avoiding agreements that do not serve U.S. national interests.** The international treaties and conventions favored by the Obama Administration—such as the New START arms control treaty with Russia, the United Nations Convention on the Law of the Sea (UNCLOS or LOST), or the Comprehensive Nuclear Test Ban Treaty (CTBT)—undermine U.S. sovereignty and threaten America's strategic superiority.

- **Strengthening alliances and establishing new coalitions.** President Obama talks about the significance of international partnerships, but partnerships will fall short if the countries with which we align share neither our values nor our goals. The problem is that many of the institutions created in the aftermath of World War II, like the U.N., are outdated and unable to respond to today's challenges. In order to spur economic development, respect for human rights, and our nation's security, the U.S. should take the lead in creating new and more effective institutions and arrangements that will enhance strong bilateral cooperation among like-minded nations.

- **Undertaking responsible arms control.** Instead of focusing on Cold War–style arms control, the United States should adopt a defensive strategic posture based on a "protect and defend" strategy that would employ both offensive and defensive forces, both conventional and nuclear, to defeat any strategic attack on the U.S. and its allies. Such a strategy would offer opportunities for mutually beneficial cooperation with Russia and allow the U.S. and Russia to reduce their operationally deployed strategic nuclear warheads without constraining missile defenses.

- **Finishing the job in Afghanistan.** The United States will sacrifice its credibility and place vital U.S. national interests at risk if it prematurely withdraws from and accepts defeat in Afghanistan. Winning in Afghanistan will prevent that nation from again being a terrorist haven and put pressure on nuclear-armed Pakistan to deal with organized terrorist groups within its borders. It will also be a crushing blow to those who support Islamist terrorism and a stern warning to all that the U.S. can and will defend its vital national interests.

- **Encouraging freedom in Iran.** The U.S. has wasted much time and effort trying to engage the Tehran regime on nuclear issues while Iran has played diplomatic games with Washington, using engagement to buy time while advancing its anti-Western agenda. Pushing back against the Iranian regime is the only way to counter Tehran's quest for regional dominance and weaken the regime's hold on its people. The United States should not only pursue tough sanctions and other actions to prevent Iran from obtaining nuclear weapons, but also rally international condemnation of Iran's human rights abuses.

- **Resetting the "reset" policy toward Russia.** The Obama Administration has agreed to significant cuts in U.S. strategic nuclear forces under New START, abandoned missile defense deployment in Poland and the Czech Republic, pursued a policy of strategic neglect in the former Soviet Union, and downplayed violations of political freedom in Russia. This is the wrong policy. While both countries have an interest in opposing Islamist radicalism and terrorism, countering proliferation, and boosting trade and investment, the United States should neither tolerate Russian geopolitical mischief nor shy away from articulating its priorities and values to Russia.

- **Standing up to China.** Over the long term, a resurgent People's Republic of China poses the greatest potential challenge to our national security. America must remain economically engaged with China and encourage free-market cooperation; develop and maintain a strong, comprehensive response against bad Chinese behavior; forge and maintain greater relations with the other nations in East Asia; and maintain a strong U.S. military presence in the region. The United States must also invest in long-range power projection systems and other systems that would counter efforts to deny U.S. forces access to the region or interfere with the freedom of the seas.

America's Cause

Without principled American leadership, the world will become a more dangerous place—for Americans and for freedom. Transnational terrorism, rampant anti-Americanism, unaccountable international institutions, nuclear proliferation, and regional conflict all represent threats to our security, our liberties, and our prosperity. The ability of rogue nations and hostile non-state actors to use weapons of mass destruction against the United States creates a new and compelling interest in America's actively defending itself.

The United States must have the will and the means to remain engaged in the world, not only to protect the nation and its citizens from freedom's adversaries, but also to defend its principles, policies, and vital interests wherever they may be threatened. A complacent America, either at home or abroad, endangers not only the peaceful and productive future of this country, but also that of its friends and allies.

Restoring Constitutional Government

MOST AMERICANS RECOGNIZE THAT OUR fiscal affairs are in grave disarray. Many are also aware that the world has grown more dangerous. Yet the most difficult task ahead—perhaps the greatest challenge we have ever faced—is to restore constitutional government in the United States.

The Constitution is central to American life. It is not simply an organizational structure. Rather, it is the arrangement that formally constitutes "We, the People" as the authority for our national government. It orders our politics, defines our nation, and protects our freedom.

The purpose of the United States Constitution is to secure the rights and liberties promised in the Declaration of Independence through an energetic national government of limited powers, focused on core functions and with the structural arrangements that preserve the consent of the governed and make the American experiment in republican government work.

Today, the federal government has acquired an all but unquestioned dominance over virtually every area of American life, acting without constitutional limits and restricted only by expediency, political will, and (less and less) budget constraints. The unlimited scope and depth of its rules means that the *federal* government increasingly regulates more and more of our most basic activities, like how much water is in our toilets and what kind of light bulbs we can buy. This is a government that is unlimited by any organizing principle, increasingly undemocratic and damaging to popular self-government.

The welfare state is deeply entrenched, and unraveling today's regulatory government will be extremely difficult. Nevertheless, the objective must be clear: to restore limits on a government that is out of control and increasingly oblivious of constitutional restraint.

Today, the federal government has acquired an all but unquestioned dominance over virtually every area of American life, acting without constitutional limits and restricted only by expediency and political will.

Rogue Justice

The rise of unlimited government is most familiar and most prominent in the form of judicial activism.

The Founders thought the judiciary would be the "least dangerous branch," but progressive judges have usurped the functions of the other two branches and transformed the courts into policymaking bodies that wield wide-ranging power. As a result, the final answer to virtually every major public policy question in America today is provided by unelected judges.

Judicial activism occurs when judges abandon their duty to interpret the Constitution and laws as written. Rather than deferring to the lawmaking role of the elected branches of government, activist judges seek to impose their own policy preferences, undermining the democratic process that is vital to our system of government.

Several egregious examples of judicial activism have occurred over the past decade:

- In *Kelo v. City of New London,* for example, the Supreme Court interpreted the Constitution to allow government to seize citizens' homes—not to build a road or fulfill some other public use but to transfer property to a private corporation in order to generate more tax revenue.

- In the "Mt. Soledad Cross" case, the United States Court of Appeals for the Ninth Circuit found that the federal government could not acquire and maintain a war memorial that included a cross honoring veterans because the court believed that such a display violated the Constitution's prohibition on Congress respecting an establishment of religion.

- In *Boumediene v. Bush,* for the first time in U.S. history, the Supreme Court bestowed a constitutional right to *habeas corpus* on alien enemies detained abroad by our military forces in the course of an ongoing war. Justice Antonin Scalia highlighted the real-world impact of the decision, noting in his dissent that the game of bait-and-switch engaged in by the Court's wartime decisions "will almost certainly cause more Americans to be killed."

- Despite our nation's great progress toward equality under the law, in *Grutter v. Bollinger,* the Supreme Court held that public institutions of higher education may engage in racial discrimination by giving members of minority groups preference "to achieve a diverse student body."

- In upholding the individual health care mandate of Obamacare, the Sixth Circuit Court of Appeals recently found that Congress, pursuant to its constitutional authority to regulate interstate commerce, could force Americans who are not engaged in commercial activity to purchase a product continuously from a private company—an interpretation that would result in an unprecedented expansion of government authority and fundamentally rewrite the Constitution's limitations.

We need learned judges who take the Constitution seriously and follow it faithfully. A constitutionalist judge interprets the laws as they are written, regardless of whether he or she personally approves of the laws or would prefer a different outcome in a particular case. Candidates and officeholders should promote robust debate regarding the importance of approving constitutionalist judges. Judicial appointments and confirmations are important opportunities for Presidents, nominees, and the Senate to advance and explain the proper role of judges and the legitimate parameters of constitutional interpretation. Most important, the President should appoint, and the Senate should use its advice and consent role to confirm, only constitutionalist judges.

The President—like judges or Members of Congress— takes an oath to uphold the Constitution in carrying out the responsibilities of his office.

An Imperial President

As a part of his reelection campaign, President Obama has launched an effort called "We Can't Wait" to highlight his actions independent of Congress. Setting aside the usual politics of a President running for reelection against Congress, this effort is built on a much more troubling idea: that the President, charged with the execution of the laws, doesn't have to wait for the lawmaking branch to make, amend, or abolish the laws but can and should act on his own. This violates the spirit—and potentially the letter—of the Constitution's separation of the legislative and executive powers of Congress and the President.

Indeed, behind this effort is a persistent pattern of disregard for the powers of the legislative branch in favor of administrative decision-making without— and often in spite of—congressional action. This Administration has issued a series of new federal rules without legislative authority:

- Even though the Democrat-controlled Senate rejected President Obama's cap-and-trade plan, his Environmental Protection Agency classified carbon dioxide, the compound that sustains vegetative life, as a pollutant so that it could regulate it under the Clean Air Act.

- Although Congress defeated the Development, Relief, and Education for Alien Minors Act (known as the DREAM Act), Immigration and Customs Enforcement has adopted enforcement parameters designed to bring about the same ends as the DREAM Act.

- After the Employee Free Choice Act—designed to bolster labor unions' dwindling membership rolls—was defeated by Congress, the National Labor Relations Board announced a rule that would implement "snap elections" for union representation, limiting employers' abilities to make their case to workers and virtually guaranteeing a higher rate of unionization at the expense of workplace democracy.

- After an Internet regulation proposal failed to make it through Congress, the Federal Communications Commission announced that it would regulate the Web anyway, even despite a federal court's ruling that it had no authority to do so.

- Although Congress consistently has barred the Department of Education from getting involved in curriculum matters, the Administration has offered waivers for the No Child Left Behind law in exchange for states adopting national education standards, all without congressional authorization.

Likewise, the Administration has often simply refused to enforce laws duly enacted by Congress:

- Since it objects to existing federal immigration laws, the Administration has decided to apply those laws selectively and actively prevent the states from enforcing those laws themselves.

- Rather than push Congress to repeal federal laws against marijuana use, the Department of Justice (DOJ) simply decided it would no longer enforce those laws.

- In a similar move with respect to the Defense of Marriage Act, DOJ announced that it would stop enforcing the law or defending it from legal challenge rather than seeking legislative recourse.

A more recent example crosses the threshold of constitutionality. The President has the power to make appointments with the advice and consent of the United States Senate. On January 12, 2012, President Obama announced that the Senate was not in session and exercised the power to make "recess appointments" of three members to the National Labor Relations Board and the head of the new Consumer Financial Protection Bureau. The problem was that these "recess appointments" were made when the Senate was not in recess at all but meeting in regular, brief sessions—the very circumstances used previously by Senate Democrats (including then-Senator Barack Obama) to block President Bush's judicial appointments. These actions not only violate the spirit of the Constitution and its structure of the separation of powers, but also circumvent the letter of the law by trampling on the Senate's responsibility of advice and consent.

There is no telling where such disregard may go next, but the trend is clear, and it leads further and further away from the constitutional rule of law.

The President has unique and powerful responsibilities in our constitutional system as chief executive officer, head of state, and commander in chief. Those powers do not include the authority to make laws or to decide which laws to enforce and which to ignore. The President—like judges or Members of Congress—takes an oath to uphold the Constitution in carrying out the responsibilities of his office. Indeed, the President takes a unique oath to "faithfully execute the Office of President of the United States" and "preserve, protect and defend the Constitution of the United States." We need a President who will defend and vigorously exert his or her legitimate powers, recognizing that those powers are not arbitrary or unlimited.

Bureaucratic Tyranny

But there is a deeper current at issue. For too long, Congress has legislated without regard to any limits on its powers. Although the Constitution vests legislative powers in Congress, the majority of "laws" are actually promulgated by agencies and bureaucracies in the guise of "regulations." As a result, key policy decisions which were previously the constitutional responsibility of elected legislators are delegated to executive branch administrators whose rules have the full force and effect of laws passed by Congress. Having passed massive, broadly written pieces of legislation with little serious deliberation, Congress is increasingly an administrative body overseeing a vast array of bureaucratic policymakers and rule-making bodies.

This new bureaucratic rule and its arbitrary discretion can be seen in the early implementation of the Patient Protection and Affordable Care Act (Obamacare). In a demonstration of its benevolent authority, even before the law fully takes effect, the Administration has granted almost 2,000 waivers (mostly for union and business friends) to its own health care regulations. Although one whole program—the Community Living Assistance Services and Supports Act, or CLASS Act, Obamacare's long-term care insurance plan—has been unilaterally cancelled as completely unworkable, it has been kept on the books for possible future implementation.

> *Although the Constitution vests legislative powers in Congress, the majority of "laws" are actually promulgated by agencies and bureaucracies in the guise of "regulations."*

We now have the first real taste of what is to come. It turns out that regulations issued pursuant to Obamacare, despite earlier denials, dictate that all insurance plans must cover, at no charge, abortion-inducing drugs, contraceptives, sterilization, and patient education and counseling for women of reproductive age. Religious employers such as Catholic hospitals, Christian schools, and faith-based pregnancy care centers will have to provide and pay for such coverage for their employees regardless of their religious beliefs. Although religious institutions vehemently objected that the proposed rule would force them to provide services that as a matter of faith they find morally objectionable, Health and Human Services issued the final rule in its entirety and without the slightest change.

This is not a one-time exception to the rule of Obamacare but the essence of the law itself. One can only imagine what life would be like when the Independent Payment Advisory Board (IPAB) begins rationing health benefits to reduce

Medicare spending. It is not merely the details in Obamacare that are the problem, but the form of governance established therein, by which unelected experts are empowered to make the rules as they go along and as they see fit.

What is happening has little to do with health care or even public policy and everything to do with the role of government in the most immediate and intimate matters of our lives. In the liberal-progressive worldview, all is subject to government control, regulatory dictate, and administrative whim.

To reverse this course, we must:

- **Dismantle the administrative state.** The Constitution creates three branches of government, yet administrative agencies and vast bureaucracies operate in practice as a headless fourth branch. Rather than spending its time micromanaging the bureaucracy through oversight, Congress should reassert its authority as the nation's legislature by refusing to delegate its power to bureaucrats and taking responsibility for all the laws (and regulations) that govern us.

- **Decentralize government.** True self-government cannot be revived without a decided reversal of administrative centralization in the United States. This requires more than merely shifting bureaucratic authority to states that are themselves bureaucratic and increasingly dependent on federal largesse. Vast areas of federal policymaking must be returned to states, local communities, neighborhoods, families, and individual citizens. The best way forward starts with practical but significant reforms that will change the federal–state dynamic in key policy matters such as health care, education, and transportation.

- **Reverse the explosion of federal criminal law.** Federal criminal law used to focus on inherently wrongful conduct: treason, murder, counterfeiting, and the like. Today, an unimaginably broad range of conduct is criminalized by scores of federal departments and agencies. The Congressional Research Service estimates these offenses to be in the "tens of thousands." Congress must halt this overcriminalization rampage and begin to eliminate vague, overbroad criminal offenses that punish individuals who without criminal intent violate one of these innumerable federal criminal offenses.

- **Require the regular review and evaluation of every major program.** Too many programs, once started, are automatically reauthorized and become part of the permanent bureaucracy. Congress should subject government programs to regular reevaluation of their authority, purpose, and effectiveness, creating an ongoing mechanism that works against the automatic expansion of government. Any program that Congress has not reauthorized should be suspended for review. Committees should not be permitted to create new programs with automatic funding or that specify minimum funding levels to circumvent the appropriations process. Likewise, to prevent the perpetuation of outdated regulations, all new regulations should include a "sunset" date on which they expire automatically unless specifically renewed.

Restoring Constitutional Government

The restoration of constitutional government will not occur all at once or across the board. Nor will it result from one judicial decision, presidential order, or comprehensive piece of legislation. This means we must think strategically, defining and pursuing a realistic path that measurably reintroduces constitutional limits by focusing government on its primary obligations, restoring its responsibility and democratic accountability, and correcting its worst excesses.

Constitutional government requires those who make, interpret, and enforce the law to be guided by the Constitution above ordinary legislation, beyond the political winds of the times. Upholding the Constitution is a responsibility of all three branches of government. After all, it is the Constitution—and not the legislature, the executive, or the courts—that is the supreme law of the land. Just as the Supreme Court must be faithful to the Constitution in interpreting the laws in cases before it, so Congress in making laws and the President in signing and then executing laws are required to do the same in the exercise of their functions. For the elected branches of government to turn their authority over to the courts—or for Congress to give its legislative powers to bureaucrats—is an abdication of both constitutional responsibility and popular consent.

One of the most important tasks of public officials is to articulate how the principles and limits of their constitutional responsibilities inform and guide their actions and the public-policy choices they make. Congressmen should do this in committee deliberations and floor debates on proposed legislation, judges in their written opinions interpreting the real meaning of the Constitution in the cases before them, and Presidents in executive orders, in legislative signing statements, and especially in official addresses.

We must recommit ourselves as a nation to the principles and policies of American constitutionalism.

In the end, the question of constitutional government can be settled only by the American people. Therefore, the path of restoring constitutional government also requires a popular constitutionalism that fosters and builds a new public consensus favoring liberty and limited government, reforming and re-shaping public policy over time to reflect a constitutional framework of limited government.

In order to get government under control—especially its skyrocketing spending and debt—and refocus it on its core functions, we must turn the healthy public sentiment of the moment, which stands against a partisan agenda to revive an activist state, into a settled and enduring political opinion about the nature and purpose of constitutional government. We must recommit ourselves as a nation to the principles and policies of American constitutionalism.

Choosing Our Future

AS RONALD REAGAN ONCE OBSERVED,

This idea that government was beholden to the people, that it had no other source of power is still the newest, most unique idea in all the long history of man's relation to man.

This is the issue of this election: Whether we believe in our capacity for self-government or whether we abandon the American Revolution and confess that a little intellectual elite in a far-distant capital can plan our lives for us better than we can plan them ourselves.

You and I are told we must choose between a left or right, but I suggest there is no such thing as a left or right. There is only an up or down. Up to man's age-old dream—the maximum of individual freedom consistent with order—or down to the ant heap of totalitarianism. Regardless of their sincerity, their humanitarian motives, those who would sacrifice freedom for security have embarked on this downward path. Plutarch warned, "The real destroyer of the liberties of the people is he who spreads among them bounties, donations, and benefits."

The Founding Fathers knew a government can't control the economy without controlling people. And they knew when a government sets out to do that, it must use force and coercion to achieve its purpose. So we have come to a time for choosing.

Almost 50 years later, the debate between the Founders' constitutionalism and the progressive paradigm is engaged, perhaps as never before, in the American mind. How that debate is resolved will determine whether the United States continues to be what President Reagan called "a shining city upon a hill."

As conservatives, our goal must be nothing less than to restore the liberating principles of America—its philosophical grounding, its constitutional wisdom, and its limitless spirit of self-government and independence—as the governing philosophy of the nation.

A conservatism of the Declaration defends life, liberty, and the pursuit of happiness. It derives legitimacy from the consent of the governed but recognizes that we must abide by "the laws of nature and nature's God."

A conservatism of the Constitution limits government's powers but makes sure that it performs its proper job effectively and energetically. It checks and balances that power in distinct branches of government and through an extended nation of states.

Though we often disagree, we must always remember that the true source of our fusion is not a mere agreement of policy convenience but the recognition of foundational principles that come from the same source of moral truth— timeless truths, deeply embedded in the American character.

Americans may have lost faith in government, but not in America, its enduring principles, or its unlimited promises.

It is our task to rededicate this country to its principles and the policies that harmonize with them and so save the American Dream, secure our nation's continuing independence, and begin the difficult work of restoring constitutional self-government.